Cicadas

by Helen Frost

Consulting Editor: Gail Saunders-Smith, Ph.D.

Consultant: Gary A. Dunn, Director of Education,
Young Entomologists' Society

Pebble Books

an imprint of Capstone Press
Mankato, Minnesota

Pebble Books are published by Capstone Press,
151 Good Counsel Drive, P.O. Box 669, Mankato, Minnesota 56002.
www.capstonepress.com

2 3 4 5 6 06 05 04 03 02

Library of Congress Cataloging-in-Publication Data
Frost, Helen, 1949–
    Cicadas/by Helen Frost.
    p. cm.—(Insects)
    Includes bibliographical references (p. 23) and index.
    ISBN 0-7368-0851-5 (hardcover)
    ISBN 0-7368-9086-6 (paperback)
    1. Cicadas—Juvenile literature. [1. Cicadas.] I. Title. II. Insects
(Mankato, Minn.)
QL527.C5 F76   2001
595.7'52—dc21   00-009665

Summary: Simple text and photographs describe the body parts and behavior
    of cicadas.

Note to Parents and Teachers

The Insects series supports national science standards on units on
the diversity and unity of life. The series shows that animals have
features that help them live in different environments. This book
describes cicadas and illustrates their body parts and habits. The
photographs support early readers in understanding the text. The
repetition of words and phrases helps early readers learn new
words. This book also introduces early readers to subject-specific
vocabulary words, which are defined in the Words to Know section.
Early readers may need assistance to read some words and to use
the Table of Contents, Words to Know, Read More, Internet Sites,
and Index/Word List sections of the book.

Table of Contents

4

Cicadas have six legs.

Cicadas have four wings.
Two long top wings cover
two short bottom wings.

small eyes

large eyes

Cicadas have two large eyes and three small eyes.

drinking tube ••••►

Cicadas have
a drinking tube.

Young cicadas are called nymphs. They can live underground for many years. Then they come above the ground.

exoskeleton

Cicada nymphs shed their exoskeletons many times as they grow.

16

Adult cicadas leave their exoskeletons on tree trunks.

Adult cicadas live
in trees and grass.

Male cicadas make
a loud buzzing sound.
The buzzing sound
attracts female cicadas.

Words to Know

buzz—a low, steady sound; male cicadas can make the loudest buzzing sound of any insect; their sounds can be heard more than one-fourth of a mile (.4 kilometer) away.

drinking tube—a mouthpart used for sucking liquid; cicadas suck sap from trees through their drinking tube.

exoskeleton—the tough or stiff structure on the outside of some animals; the exoskeleton covers and protects the animal.

female—an animal that can give birth to young animals or lay eggs

nymph—a young form of an insect; nymphs change into adults by shedding their skin many times; cicada nymphs live underground for 2 to 17 years.

wing—a movable part of an insect that helps it fly; most cicadas have four transparent wings.

Read More

Clyne, Densey. *Cicada Sing-Song.* Nature Close-ups. Milwaukee: Gareth Stevens, 1998.

Miller, Sara Swan. *Cicadas and Aphids: What They Have in Common.* Animals in Order. New York: Franklin Watts, 1999.

Wilsdon, Christina. *National Audobon Society First Field Guide: Insects.* New York: Scholastic, 1998.

Internet Sites

FactHound offers a safe, fun way to find Internet sites related to this book. All of the sites on FactHound have been researched by our staff.

Here's how:

1. Visit *www.facthound.com*

2. Type in this special code **0736808515** for age-appropriate sites. Or enter a search word related to this book for a more general search.

3. Click on the **Fetch It** button.

FactHound will fetch the best sites for you!

Index/Word List

Word Count: 87
Early-Intervention Level: 13

Editorial Credits

Mari C. Schuh, editor; Timothy Halldin, cover designer; Kia Bielke, production
   designer; Kimberly Danger, photo researcher

Photo Credits

A. B. Sheldon, 10
Bill Beatty, 6, 12
James P. Rowan, 20
M. H. Sharp, 1
Rob & Ann Simpson, 8, 14
Visuals Unlimited/Richard Thom, cover; Gustav Verderber, 4; Gary Meszaros, 16, 18

24